EDGE
BOOKS™

ALL
ABOUT
DOGS

NEWFOUNDLANDS

by Charlotte Wilcox

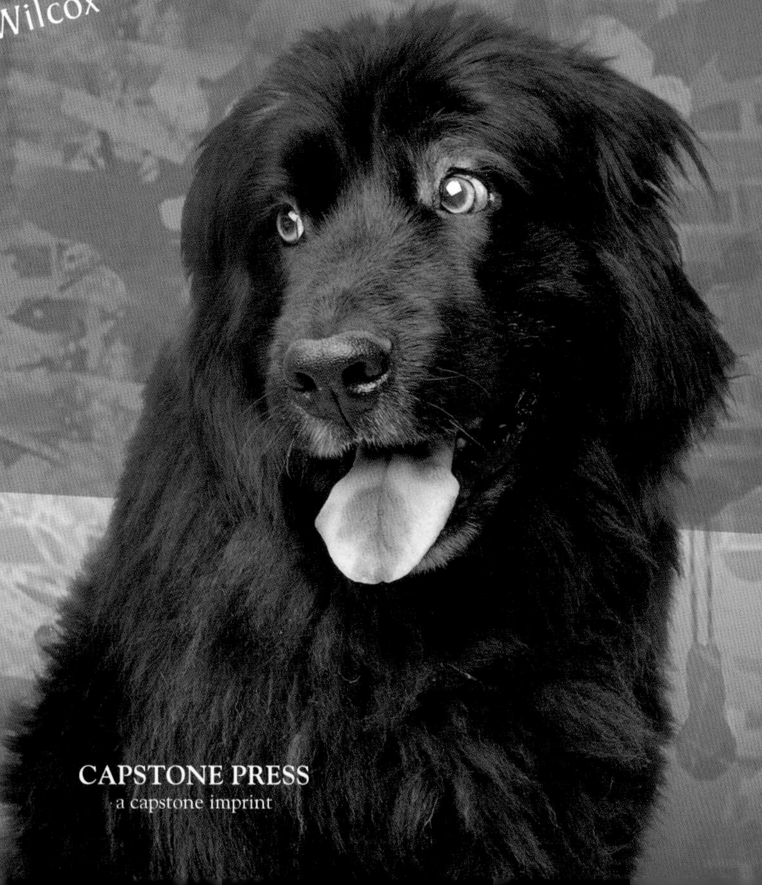

CAPSTONE PRESS
a capstone imprint

Library of Congress Cataloging-in-Publication Data
Wilcox, Charlotte.
  Newfoundlands / by Charlotte Wilcox.
    p. cm. — (Edge books. all about dogs.)
  Includes bibliographical references and index.
  Summary: "Describes the history, physical features, temperament, and care
of the Newfoundland dog breed"—Provided by publisher.
  ISBN 978-1-4296-7714-1 (library binding)
  1. Newfoundland dog—Juvenile literature. I. Title.
  SF429.N4W554 2012
  636.73—dc22

                                    2011011864

Editorial Credits
Kathryn Clay and Mari Bolte, editors; Sarah Bennett, designer; Marcie Spence,
    media researcher; Eric Manske, production specialist

Photo Credits
123RF: Isabel Poulin, 25; Alamy Images: Dave Porter, 19, imagebroker, 29,
katewarn images, 23 (bottom), Sorin Papuc, 21; Ardea: Rolf Kopfle, 6; Corbis:
Lake County Museum, 10, National Geographic Society, 16, Shannon Stapleton/
Reuters, 27; fotolia: Callalloo Canis, 11; Getty Images, Inc.: Robert E. Lougheed/
National Geographic, 9; Kimball Stock: J. Harrison, 13; Nature Picture Library:
Rob Cousins, 23 (top); Shutterstock: Daniel Gale, 14, Eric Isselee, 26, Erik Lam,
cover, 1, Joy Brown, 5, Julia Remezova, 15, Liliya Kulianionak, 7

Printed in the United States of America in Stevens Point, Wisconsin.
122011   006527WZVMI

Table of Contents

CHAPTER 1

BUILT FOR HARD WORK

Hunting dogs chase birds by **instinct**. Herding dogs round up livestock by instinct. Newfoundland dogs have a different instinct—they can save people's lives.

Instinct tells Newfoundlands what to do in dangerous situations. The Newfoundland is the only breed that has natural lifesaving ability listed in its American Kennel Club (AKC) **breed standard**.

Newfoundlands' body features help them save lives. These dogs are one of the largest and strongest breeds. They have good eyesight and hearing.

Many Newfoundlands are excellent swimmers. They have two layers of hair. The inner layer is soft and fuzzy. The outer layer is long and sleek. Water does not go through the outer layer. This layer keeps Newfoundlands' skin dry when they swim. Newfoundlands also have webbed feet. The extra skin connecting their toes helps make them good swimmers.

instinct—behavior that is natural rather than learned

breed standard—the physical features of a breed that judges look for in a dog show

Finding a Newfoundland

It is best to buy Newfoundland puppies from breeders. Pet stores sometimes sell dogs with health problems. Responsible breeders are very picky about which dogs they breed. They want to produce healthy, friendly puppies.

Choose a puppy with a personality that fits your own. A lively puppy will make a good pet for an active person. If you like to sit quietly in your spare time, a mellow puppy may be best. Keep in mind that all Newfies need activity and quality time with their owners.

Newfoundland litters can vary in size, from two to 15 puppies.

You also may be able to adopt an adult Newfoundland through a rescue group or animal shelter. Many healthy, loving Newfoundlands are abandoned each year.

EDGE FACT

Newfoundlands have been described as "gentle giants."

CHAPTER 2

NEWFOUNDLAND HISTORY

The early history of Newfoundland and its dogs is not clear. The first people to live on what is now the island of Newfoundland were native North Americans. Historians think these native peoples first lived on the island thousands of years ago. They were related to today's Inuit people. Inuit people now live in Alaska, Canada, Greenland, and Siberia.

Inuit people have raised dogs for thousands of years. They use Siberian husky dogs to hunt, pull, and carry things. Some people think the Siberian husky is one **ancestor** of the Newfoundland.

EDGE FACT

Newfoundland dogs are named after the island of Newfoundland. The island is located off the eastern coast of Canada's mainland.

Norse People

Historians also think that Newfoundlands are related to Norse dogs. The Norse people arrived in Newfoundland about 1,000 years ago. The Norse people came from the area that is now Scandinavia. This area includes Norway, Sweden, Denmark, Iceland, and Greenland.

Newfoundlands are natural-born swimmers.

ancestor—a family member who lived a long time ago

Leif Eriksson reached
Newfoundland
around AD 1000.

Some Norse sailors had tried to sail from Iceland to
Greenland in AD 986. But a giant storm blew their ship
off course. These sailors landed on what is now the island
of Newfoundland.

These Norse sailors returned to Iceland after the storm.
They told other people about the island. The explorer
Leif Eriksson heard these stories. He wanted to visit
this island. He and his men were the first Europeans
to explore Newfoundland.

Some Norse people decided to move to the island. They brought their families, livestock, and dogs with them. The Norse dogs had thick hair to protect them from cold weather. Their hair came in many color combinations. Many of them had white markings. Others were all black. The Norse dogs mated with the dogs that belonged to the native people of the island.

Newfoundlands can be black, brown, gray, and a combination of white and black.

More European Visitors

Fishermen from Spain also traveled to Newfoundland about 1,000 years ago. They visited the island after the Norse people lived there. The Spanish fishermen did not stay on the island. They caught fish and took them back to Spain to sell. These fishermen noticed the native dogs. They also brought their own dogs to the island.

The dogs from Spain were called Mastiffs. These large, heavy dogs are native to Europe and Asia. They are ancestors of many large breeds. Mastiffs bred with native and Norse dogs on Newfoundland.

Explorers from England first came to Newfoundland in 1497. Captain John Cabot claimed the island as territory for England. He named the area Newfoundland from his description of the territory as "new founde lande."

English people moved to the island in the late 1500s. Newfoundland soon became an important world fishing center.

Newfoundlands were bred to be working dogs.

The Newfoundland's layered coat is water-resistant.

Fishermen's Dogs

Dogs were important on fishing boats. They helped fishermen with the nets used to catch fish. The nets hung from ropes into the water. Fish swam into the nets. The fishermen pulled the ropes to move the nets onto the boats. Dogs helped pull ropes and nets with their mouths. The dogs also used their mouths to catch escaping fish in shallow water.

Ships from many countries sailed to the island of Newfoundland. Sailors and passengers saw how helpful the native dogs were. Soon ships from many countries had a Newfie on board. These big dogs went on to live all over the world.

Newfoundlands worked on ships from about 1600 to 1900. They were good dogs to have aboard ships because they could swim well. They were also intelligent and strong. They could carry heavy ropes and pull nets.

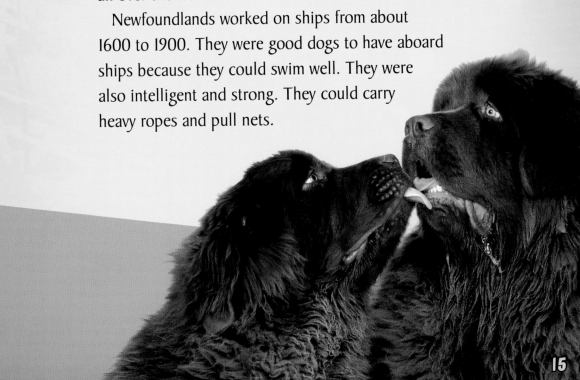

Running the Lifeline

Newfoundlands had one especially important job. They carried a rope called a lifeline to shore. Sailors used lifelines when a ship was in danger of sinking near land. The lifeline made it possible for the people to reach solid ground. The water was too cold and rough for a person to swim to shore during a storm. But a Newfoundland could do it.

The dogs were well suited to running the lifeline. They were very brave and very strong. Their big, powerful swimming strokes could propel them through giant waves. Newfoundlands could see in even murky water. They also swam well in the dark.

Newfoundland dogs rescued hundreds of people by carrying lifelines. Other times they carried people to shore one at a time. People would grip the Newfoundlands' long hair. Sometimes Newfoundlands even pulled small boats to shore.

Newfoundlands used their strong bodies to pull shipwreck victims to shore.

CHAPTER 3

LARGE AND PLAYFUL

Newfoundlands are hard to miss. Their giant bodies usually attract a lot of attention. Their size might even cause some people to be afraid of them. But there's no reason to be afraid of these dogs. Newfoundlands are gentle and playful.

Appearance

Male Newfoundlands stand about 28 inches (71 centimeters) tall. Females stand about 26 inches (66 cm) tall. Height is measured from the ground to the **withers**.

Males generally weigh between 130 and 150 pounds (59 and 68 kilograms). Females usually weigh between 100 and 120 pounds (45 and 54 kg).

Most Newfoundlands are solid black, brown, or gray. Some of these solid-colored dogs have white areas on their chins, chests, toes, or the tips of their tails.

withers—the top of an animal's shoulders

In Europe Landseer Newfoundlands are recognized as their own breed.

Newfies also can be white with black markings. This color is called Landseer. It is named for Sir Edwin Henry Landseer. Landseer was a famous London artist who painted pictures of Newfoundlands in the 1800s. Landseer Newfoundlands have a large black patch over their backs. Another black patch covers their rears and part of their tails. A Landseer's head is either all black or black and white.

EDGE FACT

Some Newfoundlands weigh more than 200 pounds (90 kilograms).

Temperament

Newfoundlands have good-natured personalities, which makes these dogs great choices as family pets. In fact, having a sweet personality is included in the Newfoundland's breed standard for the AKC. Newfies get along well with children, and some are protective over children.

Newfoundlands are also intelligent and can be easily trained. Because of the Newfie's background, some people train their Newfoundlands to save lives. These dogs can search for lost people, rescue people from drowning, or find people buried under snow.

One national search-and-rescue group used only Newfoundlands. The Black Paws Search, Rescue, and Avalanche Academy formed in 1985 in Big Fork, Montana. The group was named Black Paws in honor of the Newfoundland dogs.

Black Paws no longer exists, but there are still many Newfoundland search-and-rescue groups in the United States. People who own Newfoundlands and want to learn about rescue work can attend training. At training, Newfoundlands and their owners learn to find people lost in wilderness areas.

Newfies make great swimming companions.

EDGE FACT

A Newfoundland once rescued 63 shipwrecked sailors.

Work and Play

Newfoundlands can do many jobs. They can carry packs on their backs or pull carts. Some Newfies wear harnesses attached to sleds. Newfoundlands can also pull people on skis. This activity is called skijoring.

Because of their large size, Newfoundlands need more exercise than most dog breeds. A simple walk around the neighborhood each day is not enough for them. Your Newfie must get lively playtime each day. If you have a fenced yard, use it to run around and play with your pet. Most Newfies enjoy playing in water. In warm weather, swimming is a great way for your Newfie to get exercise.

Many Newfoundland owners hike with their dogs. The dogs' large webbed feet provide support on rough ground. They can hike for many hours.

EDGE FACT

People once trained Newfoundlands to walk on treadmills to power machines.

Newfies are born with a love for water.

23

CHAPTER 4

CARING FOR A NEWFOUNDLAND

Newfoundlands are generally easy to care for. But new owners must be prepared to own a member of this large breed. Newfies grow quickly. These dogs are fully grown within a year. Newfoundlands also shed a great deal of hair and drool, so they need regular grooming.

Feeding a Newfoundland

Like all dogs, the best type of food for Newfoundlands is good-quality, ready-prepared dog food. The amount of food dogs need depends on their age and activity level. It is important to feed dogs only the amount of food they need. Overweight dogs often develop health problems.

Grown Newfoundlands may eat 24 to 32 ounces (680 to 907 grams) of food each day. It is best to divide the food into two meals to help with digestion.

Dogs need plenty of water each day. Fresh water should be available to them at all times.

Some foods are dangerous for dogs. Don't give your dog spicy or fatty foods. Small or sharp bones can injure dogs' stomachs. Fish and chicken bones are especially unsafe for dogs.

Grooming

You should brush your Newfoundland every day to keep its long hair from getting tangled. Newfoundlands shed a little hair every day. They shed large amounts once or twice a year. They need extra brushing during those times. Because Newfoundlands have so much hair, they need to be bathed regularly. Dog shampoo can be purchased at a pet supply store. Never use your own shampoo on your Newfie. It can dry out your dog's skin.

Newfoundlands should be groomed well before being bathed to keep the dogs' fur from matting.

Your Newfoundland's toenails should be kept short. Long toenails can cause foot problems in large breeds. Trim your Newfoundland's nails every two or three weeks. If you can hear your dog's nails when it walks, your pet is overdue for a clipping.

Your Newfie's teeth also need to be brushed often. Like its shampoo, your dog's toothpaste must be made only for dogs. Human toothpaste can make your pet sick.

Health Care

Newfoundlands need to visit a veterinarian each year. The vet will weigh your dog, take its temperature, and check its joints. The vet will give **vaccinations** to guard your dog from illnesses. He or she will also check for signs of any physical problems.

Some health problems are more common in Newfoundlands than in other dogs. Newfies can suffer from hip dysplasia. This disease keeps a dog's hips from fitting together properly. Hip dysplasia causes pain and makes movement difficult.

If you don't plan to breed your Newfoundland, you should have your vet spay or neuter your dog. These simple operations prevent dogs from having puppies. Having your dog spayed or neutered helps reduce the pet population. It also lowers your dog's chances of getting diseases, including some types of cancer.

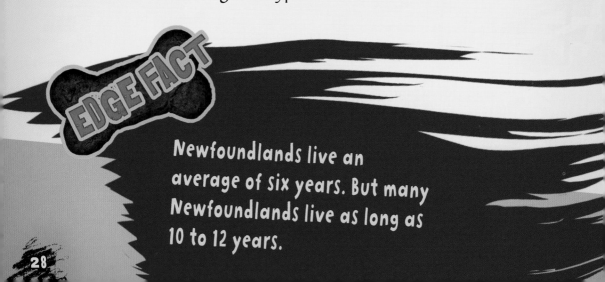

EDGE FACT

Newfoundlands live an average of six years. But many Newfoundlands live as long as 10 to 12 years.

A Loyal Pet

Taking proper care of your Newfoundland will keep your pet happy and healthy. These smart and loyal animals require a lot of time and care. From feeding to exercising, caring for a Newfie will be a big part of each day. But the care and attention you give your dog will be worth it. Maybe this gentle giant might even save your life one day.

vaccination—a shot of medicine that protects animals from a disease

Glossary

ancestor (AN-ses-tuhr)—a family member who lived long ago

breeder (BREE-duhr)—someone who breeds and raises dogs or other animals

breed standard (BREED STAN-derd)—the physical features of a breed that judges look for in a dog show

instinct (IN-stinkt)—a behavior that animals do naturally; an instinct is not learned

neuter (NOO-tur)—to operate on a male animal so it is unable to produce young

spay (SPAY)—to operate on a female animal so it is unable to produce young

vaccination (vak-suh-NAY-shun)—a shot of medicine that protects animals from a disease

withers (WITH-urs)—the top of an animal's shoulders; a dog's height is measured from the ground to the withers

Read More

Gagne, Tammy. *Dog Care: Feeding Your Pup a Healthy Diet and Other Dog Care Tips.* Dog Ownership. Mankato, Minn.: Capstone Press, 2012.

Landau, Elaine. *Newfoundlands Are the Best!* Best Dogs Ever. Minneapolis: Lerner, 2011.

Wheeler, Jill C. *Newfoundlands.* Checkerboard Animal Library. Dogs VIII. Edina, Minn.: ABDO, 2010.

Internet Sites

FactHound offers a safe, fun way to find Internet sites related to this book. All of the sites on FactHound have been researched by our staff.

Here's all you do:

Visit *www.facthound.com*

Type in this code: 9781429677141

Check out projects, games and lots more at
www.capstonekids.com

Index